Running 1 Change:

Embracing Menopause and Finding Power in Every Step.

BY

Claire Kyriacou

This disclaimer applies to any loss, damages or injury caused by the use and application, whether directly or indirectly, of any advice or information presented, whether for breach of contract, tort, negligence, personal injury, criminal intent, or under any other cause of action.

You agree to accept all risks of using the information presented inside this book.

You agree that by continuing to read this book, where appropriate and/or necessary, you shall consult a professional (including but not limited to your doctor, attorney, or financial advisor or such other advisor as needed) before using any of the suggested remedies, techniques, or information in this book.

Table of Contents

Contents

Introduction

Allow me to introduce myself. I'm Claire, a wife, a mother, a full time Receptionist at a Special Needs School and a Mum who likes to run. I have two beautiful children, two amazing stepdaughters and two adorable grandsons. I have been with my husband for over 20 years and in that time, we have created our perfect life. A lovely home in Surrey, a couple of exotic holidays a year and a wonderful circle of close friends. We own an old VW campervan that has recently undergone renovation, and we now spend our weekends away with friends, camping in the UK and France. Life is good!! So when I started to notice changes, I couldn't work out what was happening. Everything in my life was picture perfect. My children were of an age where life was getting easier. My husband and I, very much in love, enjoying each other's company and making plans for the next stage in our lives. Having more time to arrange date nights or weekends away. I have a job that I genuinely love, which is a gift, to wake up every morning knowing you are going to spend 8 hours in a place that you love and enjoy is a rare find, so what was wrong? Why was I feeling the way I was? It seemed alien to my nature. I've always been the happy-go-lucky type, carefree and easy-going, never one to take life too seriously. Yet here I was, grappling with these emotions I couldn't quite understand. Deep down, I knew the issue resided within me, but pinpointing it proved elusive. My instinct was to point fingers elsewhere, to blame external factors and other people for my inner turmoil.

I had heard the term "perimenopause" tossed around by a few friends and even heard celebrities discussing it on radio and TV. It seemed like everywhere I turned; someone was mentioning it.

However, back then, at 44 years old, I didn't pay it much attention. In my eyes, I was going to be forever young. I know now that women can go through perimenopause at a much younger age but at the time I associated menopause with old women, those going through "the change", and it didn't seem like something that would affect someone as young as me. Oh, how wrong I was!

In the early years, the signs were subtle: a few night sweats, itchy skin, a bit moody just before a period, occasionally snapping at my husband over trivial things. Moments of anxiety and worry but nothing to suggest I needed to seek help.

It was in my late 40's when everything changed dramatically. Like countless other women, I found myself navigating the turbulent waters of perimenopause. The transition brought about a whirlwind of physical and emotional changes that I struggled to come to terms with. I had no idea what was going on, I just knew that I was different. Feeling like a stranger to myself, I wrestled with mood swings, tears, anxiety, anger and an overwhelming sense of impending doom. Laughter seemed a distant memory, replaced by a cocktail of loneliness, insecurity, impostor syndrome, and an inexplicable lack of motivation. By the close of 2021, I had hit rock bottom emotionally, recognising the urgent need for assistance. Thankfully, I found solace in an empathetic GP who prescribed hormone replacement therapy (HRT). While I initially hoped for a swift resolution to my symptoms, reality proved otherwise. I understood that while HRT could alleviate some of my struggles, true healing required more than just medication. Little did I realise, the key to my salvation lay right at my feet, quite literally. It was through stumbling upon running that I discovered a powerful tool to navigate and triumph over the challenges of perimenopause.

When I first considered running, it seemed like a mammoth task. As a woman who had never thought of herself as a runner, I was hesitant to take on the challenge of pounding the pavement for miles. However, as I put on my running shoes and took my first steps, I realised that running was more than just a way to stay fit. It was a way for me to take control of my body and mind during a time of significant change.

I've never been someone who enjoys my own company, I would rather "keep busy" than sit and chill out. I'd clean, hoover, potter, anything but just relax. My journey into running has revealed that occasionally, we do require moments of solitude, separate from our home, work, children, and partners, to delve into our own thoughts and gain clarity. And that's OK. While running, I've experienced every emotion imaginable - from tears to laughter, from inner debates to moments of dancing and singing. Through it all, I've rediscovered a piece of myself, thanks to the profound connection I find in running.

I am confident that if I, starting as a complete beginner, could progress to the point of completing my second marathon in my late 40's, then anyone has the potential to embrace running and become a runner.

This book is specifically designed to encourage women to adopt running as a means of dealing with the various challenges that come with menopause. It doesn't matter if you're currently experiencing perimenopausal symptoms or are already in the throes of menopause; running can be a powerful tool to aid you in your quest for a healthy and balanced life. By engaging in regular running, you can experience a wide range of physical and mental benefits that can help you go through the often-difficult transition into menopause, helping you to feel better, more energised, and more in control. So, whether you're an experienced runner or just starting out, this book can help you harness the power of running to overcome the unique challenges of this time in your life.

In the following pages, we'll take a closer look at the many ways in which running can benefit women who are going through menopause. We'll explore the physical and mental advantages of this activity, from the strength and stamina gained through training to the emotional resilience that comes from spending time in nature. But this book is more than just a call to action for you to put on your running shoes and hit the pavement, although I do highly recommend it! It's a comprehensive guide, packed with helpful tips and strategies on how to get started, stay motivated, and overcome obstacles along the way.

Whether you're a complete novice or a seasoned runner looking for new challenges, I invite you to join me on this journey. Together, we'll discover how running can help you not only cope with menopause but also thrive in the midst of it.

Chapter 1

Understanding Perimenopause and Menopause

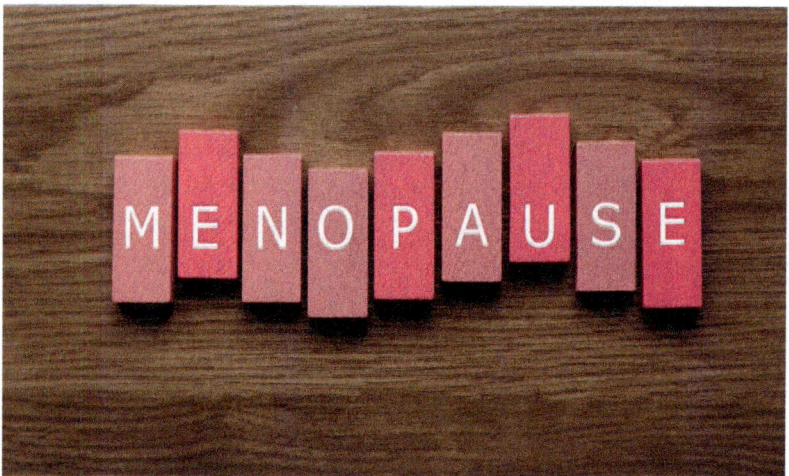

Key Terms and Definitions

Perimenopause and Menopause are natural stages in a woman's life, but the terminology and notions surrounding them can sometimes feel like a maze. Let's start by clarifying the meaning of these terms:

Perimenopause: This is the transition period leading to menopause. It can begin in women in their 40's or even earlier and is marked by hormonal change and alterations in the menstrual cycle. This transition period can last for several years, with symptoms varying in intensity and duration from woman to woman. Although it's not technically menopause, perimenopause signals that it's approaching. It's important for women experiencing perimenopause to seek support and guidance from healthcare professionals to manage symptoms effectively. Lifestyle modifications, such as regular exercise, a balanced diet, stress reduction techniques, and adequate sleep, can help alleviate some symptoms. Hormone therapy or other medications may also be prescribed to relieve severe symptoms or complications associated with perimenopause.

Menopause: Menopause is a time, usually occurring in the late 40's or early 50's, when a woman has not had a period for 12 consecutive months. The ovaries gradually decrease their production of the hormones oestrogen and progesterone, leading to a cessation of menstrual cycles and fertility. This marks the end of the reproductive years. This hormonal shift can result in a variety of physical and emotional symptoms, which can vary in severity and duration from woman to woman. Hormone therapy (HT), also known as hormone replacement therapy (HRT), involves taking oestrogen alone or in combination with progesterone to alleviate symptoms such as hot flashes, vaginal dryness, and bone loss. However, HRT is not suitable for everyone and may carry certain risks, so it's important to discuss the potential benefits and risks with a healthcare provider. Other non-hormonal medications, lifestyle modifications, and alternative therapies such as herbal supplements, acupuncture, and cognitive-behavioural therapy may also be helpful in managing menopausal symptoms.

Hormonal changes and their effects

A key aspect of perimenopause and menopause is the change in hormonal balance in a woman's body. The main hormones involved include oestrogen and progesterone, which have far-reaching effects on various bodily functions. Understanding these changes is critical to steering this period:

Oestrogen: This hormone plays a central role in regulating the menstrual cycle, bone density, and the health of the reproductive organs. As you enter menopause, oestrogen levels decline, leading to a series of physical and emotional changes. There are several types of oestrogen, but the primary ones in women are oestradiol, the primary form of oestrogen in your body during your reproductive years. It's the most potent form of oestrogen. Oestrone, the primary form of oestrogen that your body makes after menopause and oestriol. These hormones are produced primarily by the ovaries before menopause, although smaller amounts are also synthesised by other tissues such as the adrenal glands and fat cells.

Progesterone: Progesterone is another hormone closely related to the menstrual cycle. During perimenopause, its levels can become abnormal, contributing to irregular menstruation, heavier or lighter periods, and other symptoms such as hot flashes, mood swings, and sleep disturbances. As menopause approaches and ovarian function decreases further, the production of both oestrogen and progesterone declines. Eventually, the ovaries stop releasing eggs altogether, leading to the end of menstrual periods and the onset of menopause. After menopause, progesterone levels remain low as the ovaries no longer produce it. However, small amounts of progesterone can still be produced by the adrenal glands and other tissues in the body.

Recognise the signs and symptoms

Perimenopause and Menopause come with a variety of signs and symptoms, both physical and mental. These can vary greatly from woman to woman.

My mental symptoms far outweighed any physical symptoms at first. Although I suffered with night sweats, itchy skin, brittle nails and thinning hair, I know right, what a catch! It was the emotional turmoil that truly tested me. Tears flowed frequently, anger simmered constantly, and irrational rage flared over trivial matters. Living with me wasn't easy; I was well aware of it, as were my family members. I became the proverbial elephant in the room, a presence impossible to ignore. I've learned now that we don't need to live feeling this way; we can make changes. It's crucial to listen to our bodies and emotions and recognise the shifts within us. The first time I spoke to a Dr she wanted to prescribe me Anti-depressants, this is quite common and I'm sure work for many women but I knew this wasn't what I needed. I knew myself well enough to know these feelings were not depression, it was something different.

There are a wide range of different symptoms. Some notable criteria include:

Irregular menstruation: Changes in the flow, length, and regularity of your menstrual cycle are usually one of the first signs of perimenopause. Changes in the amount of blood flow during menstruation can also be considered irregular. This can include unusually heavy bleeding or very light bleeding. Sometimes, individuals might skip periods entirely.

Hot flashes and night sweats: Sudden hot flashes, sweating and reddening of the skin, mainly on the face, neck, and chest usually accompanied by a rapid heartbeat and a feeling of flushing. They are caused by hormonal changes, particularly a decrease in oestrogen levels, which affects the body's temperature regulation.

Mood swings and emotional changes: Hormonal changes can lead to irritability, mood changes, and feelings of sadness or anxiety. Understanding the multifaceted nature of mood swings and emotional changes during perimenopause can empower women to seek appropriate support and implement effective coping strategies to navigate this chapter with greater ease.

Vaginal and urinary changes: Dryness, sexual discomfort, and urinary tract symptoms may happen. Declining oestrogen levels can result in decreased vaginal lubrication, leading to vaginal dryness. This can cause discomfort, itching, and pain during intercourse. Vaginal dryness may also increase the risk of vaginal infections.

Sleep disorders: Many women have sleep challenges, such as insomnia or waking up frequently at night. Difficulty falling asleep, staying asleep, or both. Hormonal fluctuations can contribute to insomnia during perimenopause, as declining levels of oestrogen and progesterone may disrupt the body's natural sleep-wake cycle. Strategies that may help improve sleep quality during perimenopause include: Creating a comfortable sleep environment that is cool, dark, and quiet. Practising relaxation techniques such as deep breathing, meditation, or yoga before bedtime. Avoiding stimulants such as caffeine and nicotine and managing stress through techniques such as mindfulness, therapy, or stress-reduction techniques.

Physical changes: These can include weight gain, skin and hair changes, and breast tissue changes. Perimenopause can affect the skin and hair due to declining levels of oestrogen. Skin may become drier, thinner, and less elastic, leading to an increase in wrinkles and sagging. Hair may become thinner and more brittle, and some women may experience hair loss or changes in hair texture. Many women also experience weight gain, particularly around the abdomen, during perimenopause. This can be due to a combination of hormonal changes, decreased metabolism, and lifestyle factors such as diet and exercise habits.

Perimenopausal Coping Strategies & Lifestyle Adaptation

Perimenopause is an intermediate period that can last several years before menopause. Thus, examining its steps is crucial to navigating this often turbulent passage.

Stages of perimenopause

Early perimenopause (premenopause): This is the first stage, which usually begins in your late 30's or early 40's. Hormone levels begin to change, leading to irregular menstrual cycles. Some women may not notice substantial changes during this period.

Mid-perimenopause: Usually occurring in your late 40's, mid-perimenopause brings more pronounced hormonal changes. Irregular menstruation becomes more severe, and common symptoms such as hot flashes, mood changes and difficulty sleeping may appear.

Late perimenopause (perimenopause): This phase marks the months or years immediately preceding menopause. Menstrual cycles become very irregular and symptoms can become severe. Hormone levels continually decrease, leading to more pronounced symptoms.

Coping strategies and lifestyle adaptation

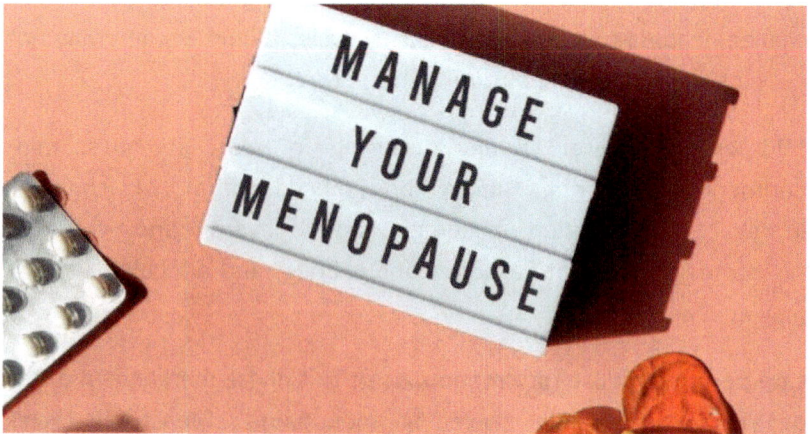

Although perimenopause has many challenges, there are effective coping strategies:

Balancing diet: A balanced diet rich in vitamin D, calcium, and phytoestrogens can help control symptoms and preserve bone health. Consuming calcium-rich foods such as dairy products (milk, yoghurt, cheese), leafy greens (kale, spinach, cabbage), tofu, almonds, and fortified foods can help maintain bone health. Omega-3 fatty acids, found in fatty fish (salmon, sardines, trout), flaxseeds, chia seeds, walnuts, and olive oil, have anti-inflammatory properties and can help reduce the risk of heart disease and support brain health. Also, Colourful fruits and vegetables are rich in vitamins, minerals, antioxidants, and phytochemicals, which support overall health and help reduce the risk of chronic diseases.

Exercise regularly: Physical activity minimises the severity of symptoms, induces sound sleep, and enhances overall health. Many women experience weight gain during menopause, regular exercise helps in managing weight by burning calories and increasing metabolism. We'll be taking a closer look at running but all movement no matter what the intensity helps to improve physical and mental well-being.

Stress management: Stress worsens symptoms; practices such as meditation, yoga or deep breathing may be beneficial. Reading, listening to an Audio book. A walk in the park or along the beach. Being out in nature is a great way to clear the mind.

Hormone therapy: In some events, hormone replacement therapy (HRT) may be prescribed to reduce severe symptoms.

Lifestyle changes: Reducing caffeine and alcohol intake, staying hydrated, and maintaining a regular sleep schedule can also help.

Accepting menopause: An inevitable stage in life

Menopause is the apex of the perimenopausal stage, marking the end of the childbearing years and making way for a new chapter. Understanding this transition is critical because it signals the cessation of menstruation for at least 12 consecutive months. While this brings challenges, it also presents opportunities for growth, self-discovery, and the wisdom that comes with age. Accepting menopause is not a matter of resignation; it's about recognising the strength and resilience within you to navigate this transition with grace and confidence.

Menopause is not a single event but a journey that begins with perimenopause, in which the body gradually adapts to hormonal changes, leading to the cessation of the menstrual cycle. This process can last for several years, during which time various symptoms may appear. While hot flashes, mood swings, and difficulty sleeping can be difficult, they also represent a changing landscape, a sign that the body is in transition. Acceptance is understanding that these changes are part of the tapestry of life, a testament to the complex and beautiful workings of the female body. It's about realising that menopause doesn't diminish your worth but rather increases your strength and resilience.

This inevitable phase of life gives you the room to reassess priorities, set new goals, and embark on new and exciting experiences. Now is the moment to prioritise self-care, nurture your physical and mental health, and assemble a strong support network. Acceptance allows you to embrace the independence that comes with the end of your monthly period, allowing you to explore life's limitless prospects.

In the grand scheme of a woman's life, menopause is a horizon filled with discernment, experience, and possibilities. Embrace it as a natural and beautiful sequence, evidence of your vigour and adaptability. See this as an occasion to grow, become the exceptional version of yourself, and enjoy the epic life that awaits you.

We've got this Ladies!!

Physical and emotional changes during menopause

Menopause brings with it a series of changes, both subtle and obvious, that affect many different facets of a woman's life. We will delve into the emotional and psychological aspects of this change, recognising the mixed emotions it can bring.

Let's review these changes:

Hormonal changes: Oestrogen and progesterone levels continue to decline, affecting everything from bone density to skin health.

Emotional changes: Mood swings, anxiety, and depression may occur.

Physical changes: It may affect weight, body mass index (BMI), hair, and skin.

Health considerations and preventive measures

With the arrival of menopause, certain health considerations have become increasingly consequential. Thus:

Hormonal changes associated with menopause can affect heart health, making preventative measures important.

The risk of osteoporosis increases.

Regular checkups and screenings become even more necessary during menopause.

Sexual function may become a common concern, though it can be managed effectively.

Positive aspects and opportunities of menopause

In addition to its challenges, menopause is a period with many positive aspects and opportunities. They may include:

Cessation of menstruation: No more periods! No more monthly cost of over-priced sanitary wear. No more trying to figure out "will I be on, on my next holiday?". Many women embrace this end of their periods as a liberating change.

Embracing New standpoint: Menopause often prompts a reassessment of life priorities and a grasp of new experiences. Many experience menopause once their children are older, leaving time to enjoy a quieter, calmer life style.

Self-discovery and mental advancement: It can be a time for introspection and personal growth, leading to a greater understanding of yourself. While some women navigate this period with ease, others may encounter challenges. Nevertheless, this evolution underscores the strength and resilience inherent in every woman.

Thriving Through Menopause and Beyond

Menopause is a stage where investing in your health is essential. Nutrition, exercise, and self-care are the foundations for a healthy, fulfilling life during menopause. Eating well and choosing a balanced diet support hormonal changes and overall health. Incorporate physical activity into your daily life to increase energy levels and maintain bone density. Prioritise self-care methods that help renew the body and nurture the soul. Understand the interdependence of body and mind and the importance of addressing both aspects.

We are fortunate to live in an era where women now confidently speak out. Menopause, once a taboo subject, is no longer kept in secrecy. From my own observations, women naturally embrace communication, eagerly exchanging stories and insights. Whether it's discussing an article we've stumbled upon, a social media influencer we follow, or a medical expert recommended by a friend, we readily share valuable information. I know for sure my daughter is sick of hearing about it, but I also know one day she'll be grateful for the knowledge I have shared. She won't have to go looking for answers; trust me, she has them. We're actively educating our daughters, sisters, and nieces about these transitions well in advance, ensuring they are prepared to navigate them with ease when the time comes.

Build a support network. Getting through menopause and the journey beyond will be easier when you have a support system. Leverage the power of close friends to provide emotional support and understanding. Discover the benefits of connecting with people with similar experiences. If necessary, seek advice from healthcare professionals or therapists. Beyond the split-second challenges and felicity of menopause, it's integral to look toward the future. Identify new ambitions and goals for this exciting stage of life. Explore the prospects and adventures that await you in postmenopausal.

Chapter 2

The Power of Running for Menopausal Women

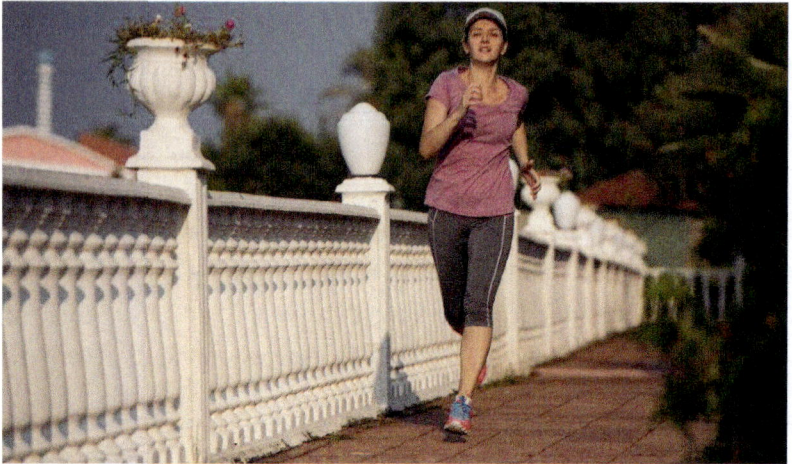

Menopause is a natural biological process that marks the end of a woman's reproductive years. During this stage, women often experience changes in their bodies that can lead to weight gain, decreased bone density, and increased risk of cardiovascular issues. However, incorporating running into your routine can be incredibly beneficial for mitigating these effects and promoting overall health and well-being.

The Benefits of running for Perimenopausal and Menopausal Women

Here are some ways in which running can help women during menopause:

Weight Management: As we age, our metabolism tends to slow down, making it easier to gain weight and harder to lose it. However, running burns calories at a high rate, making it an excellent tool for weight management. A 30-minute run can burn approximately 300-400 calories, which can help women maintain a healthy weight and prevent weight gain. Additionally, running engages multiple muscle groups, including large ones like the quadriceps, hamstrings, and glutes. Building and maintaining muscle mass through running can help boost metabolism and increase calorie burn even when at rest.

Bone Health: Menopause is often associated with a decrease in oestrogen levels, which can lead to a loss of bone density and an increased risk of osteoporosis. However, weight-bearing exercises like running can help maintain and even increase bone density. When you run, the impact of your feet hitting the ground stimulates bone cells to build new tissue, making your bones stronger and more resilient. Regular running can therefore help reduce the risk of fractures and other bone-related issues associated with menopause.

Cardiovascular Health: Menopause is also a time when women may experience changes in their cardiovascular health, including increases in blood pressure and cholesterol levels. Running is an excellent way to improve cardiovascular fitness and reduce these risk factors. Running strengthens the heart muscle, improves circulation, and helps lower blood pressure and cholesterol levels. It also increases lung capacity and improves oxygen uptake, leading to better overall cardiovascular health. Additionally, running can help reduce the risk of developing chronic diseases such as heart disease, stroke, and type 2 diabetes, which become more prevalent during and after menopause.

Thus, incorporating running into your routine during menopause can have numerous physical benefits, including weight management, improved bone health, and better cardiovascular fitness. By making running a regular part of your lifestyle, you can not only manage the negative effects of menopause but also improve your overall health and quality of life.

The Mental Health Benefits of Running During Menopause

Menopause is a challenging phase for women, both physically and mentally. Thankfully, running can be an excellent tool to manage the various symptoms of menopause. Here are some of the many mental health benefits of running:

Stress Reduction: Running is a great way to relieve stress and tension. The rhythmic motion of running, combined with the release of endorphins, can significantly reduce feelings of stress and anxiety. Moreover, focusing on your breathing and the rhythm of your footsteps can help clear your mind and promote relaxation. While running, I often find myself immersed in an audiobook or podcast, effortlessly losing track of time. Whether it's a gripping thriller or a captivating romance novel, the experience not only clears my mind but also has the power to make me forget that I'm even running.

Mood Improvement: Research has shown that regular running can improve mood and overall emotional well-being. The endorphins released during exercise act as natural mood lifters, helping to alleviate symptoms of depression and boost feelings of happiness and contentment. Even a short run can leave you feeling more energised and positive, making it an excellent tool for managing mood swings during menopause. Meeting up with a friend for a jog around the block and chatting about your day can lift your spirits.

Increased Confidence: Engaging in regular physical activity like running can boost self-esteem and confidence levels. As you set and achieve running goals, you'll gain a sense of accomplishment and pride in your abilities. Over time, this can translate into increased confidence in other areas of your life, empowering you to tackle challenges with resilience and self-assurance. Using apps like Strava can provide valuable insight into your progress, illustrating just how much you're improving and how far you've come. Despite feeling like

31

running isn't getting any easier, the data might reveal that you've actually covered more distance or achieved a faster pace compared to the previous week. Witnessing your progress presented in black and white or on a chart can significantly boost confidence.

Mental Clarity and Focus: Running can help clear your mind and improve mental clarity, allowing you to better focus on tasks and make decisions. The meditative aspects of running, such as focusing on your breathing and surroundings, can promote mindfulness and present-moment awareness, helping you let go of worries and distractions.

Sense of Community and Connection: Running can also foster community and connection, especially if you participate in group runs or join a running club. Sharing the running experience with others can provide support, encouragement, and camaraderie, reducing feelings of isolation and loneliness that sometimes accompany menopause.

By incorporating running into your regular routine, you can strengthen your mind-body connection and enhance your overall well-being during the challenging phase of menopause.

The Importance of Exercise During Menopause

Menopause is a transitional phase in a woman's life that can be challenging both physically and mentally. Fortunately, exercise can help alleviate many of the symptoms associated with menopause such as boredom, sluggishness, feelings of laziness, and low self-esteem. Here are some key reasons why exercise is important during menopause:

Hormonal Balance: During menopause, hormone levels, including oestrogen and progesterone, undergo significant changes. Regular exercise can help regulate these hormones by stimulating the production of endorphins, which can help alleviate symptoms such as mood swings, irritability, and anxiety.

Weight Management: Menopause often brings about changes in metabolism and body composition, making weight management more challenging. Exercise, particularly aerobic activities like running, cycling, or swimming, helps burn calories and build lean muscle mass, aiding in weight maintenance or loss.

Bone Health: Declining oestrogen levels during menopause can lead to decreased bone density and an increased risk of osteoporosis. Weight-bearing exercises, including running and strength training, help strengthen bones and reduce the risk of fractures by stimulating bone formation and density.

Cardiovascular Health: Menopause is associated with an increased risk of heart disease and other cardiovascular conditions. Regular exercise, especially aerobic activities like running, improves cardiovascular health by strengthening the heart muscle, lowering blood pressure, reducing LDL cholesterol levels, and improving circulation.

Mood Regulation: Exercise has been shown to have a positive impact on mood and mental well-being, reducing symptoms of depression, anxiety, and stress. The release of endorphins during exercise can elevate mood, boost energy levels, and promote feelings of happiness and relaxation.

Cognitive Function: Exercise has cognitive benefits, including improved memory, concentration, and overall brain function. Regular physical activity has been linked to a reduced risk of cognitive decline and dementia later in life, making it an essential component of maintaining brain health during menopause.

Quality of Sleep: Menopausal symptoms such as hot flashes, night sweats, and mood disturbances can disrupt sleep patterns. Regular exercise has been shown to improve sleep quality and duration, leading to better overall health and well-being.

In summary, exercise is crucial for promoting overall well-being during menopause by supporting hormonal balance, managing weight, maintaining bone health, improving cardiovascular function, regulating mood, enhancing cognitive function, and promoting quality sleep. Incorporating regular exercise into your routine can help alleviate menopausal symptoms and improve your physical and mental health, allowing you to thrive during this phase of life.

Chapter 3

Getting Started with Running: Overcoming Challenges

Many years ago, I vividly recall my husband inviting me to join him for a run. The memory still brings a smile to my face, though at the time, it was far from a pleasant experience. Struggling to catch my breath, I couldn't even make it to the end of the road. In that moment, I harboured a strong aversion to running, convinced it was not meant for me—never had been, never would be. The sensation of being out of breath was enough to solidify my decision: I declared to myself that I would never be a runner, emphatically stating, "Not me, not ever!" However, time has a funny way of changing perspectives. Some-time later, I decided to give it another shot, this time on my own terms. Embracing a gentler approach, I began with a simple routine of run-walk intervals, progressing from one lamp post to the next. Gradually, something remarkable happened... I started to enjoy it. As I focused on the rhythm of my steps and the path stretching out before me, the discomfort of breathlessness faded into the background. With each stride, I discovered a newfound sense of freedom and joy, realising that maybe, just maybe, being a runner wasn't so far-fetched after all.

I understand starting to run can be difficult, especially when you're facing challenges that can slow you down. To make progress, it's important to take things step by step. This chapter is all about helping you overcome challenges that might be getting in the way of your goals. I want to share some practical advice that can make it easier for you to succeed, even when things seem tough. So, read on to learn how you can tackle challenges head-on and come out on top! If you're new to running and want to achieve your fitness goals, I've got some pointers that can help you gain the confidence you need to get started. By following these tips, you'll be on your way to success in no time.

Frequently Encountered Challenges In Starting Running

When I first started running, I'd slip out early on a Sunday morning, leaving before my husband and children had even woken, dedicating 30 minutes to practising my run-walk technique. As time passed, my stamina grew—I found myself running for 40 minutes, then 45, until eventually, I was effortlessly running for a full hour. The remarkable thing? No one even noticed I was gone! It dawned on me that as women, we often feel indispensable at home, but in reality, the household manages just fine without us, even if breakfast is a little later or the kids might have to make their own. It's just one morning, one precious hour in the week that's entirely ours. Despite the nagging Mum guilt, the necessity for women to carve out this time for ourselves during this stage of life is undeniable.

I'm not suggesting for a moment that you leave small children to fend for themselves while you go off and run for hours. However, if you can carve out some time to do something for yourself, it not only benefits you physically but also mentally. When we're in a better place mentally, we're better equipped to handle the everyday struggles life throws at us.

I know it's not always possible to have that alone time out so when my son was younger, that delightful age when they're still eager to be seen out with you, he would often join me for a bike ride while I went for a run. Riding alongside me, we'd chat about our day, enjoying the precious moments together. It was a perfect combination: I could get my exercise in, he could burn off some of his boundless energy, and we could bond over shared experiences.

As the evenings grew darker, he took on the role of guiding us with the lights on his bike, relishing in his newfound responsibility like my own personal bodyguard. Once he became familiar with the routes, he'd eagerly race ahead, wanting to lead the way. However, there were times when his enthusiasm carried him too far, and my attempts to catch up became a challenge.

Trying to match his speed while maintaining my pace became increasingly difficult. I didn't want to discourage him from joining me or hold him back, but I also couldn't risk pushing myself to the point of exhaustion or vomiting in the street, no one wants to see that. So, we devised a solution: I wore one earpiece of my Bluetooth headphones, and he wore the other. He would cycle ahead of me but as soon as the music stopped in his ear, he knew he was out of range and it was time to stop and wait for me to catch up. Once the music resumed, he was free to zoom off again.

This arrangement gave him the freedom he craved while providing me with the reassurance that he wouldn't venture too far. Those runs together became cherished memories for both of us. I took pride in knowing that he was witnessing his mother become fitter and faster, and I believed then, as I still do now, that children learn by example. By incorporating exercise into our daily lives and showing him that it can be enjoyable, I hoped to instil in him the importance of staying active and healthy.

If you're just starting out with running and aiming to reach your fitness targets, I've got some pointers to boost your confidence and kick start your journey. With these tips, you'll be well on your way to achieving success quickly.

Lack of Time: For many women out there, starting a running routine can prove to be quite a challenge due to their busy schedules. With work, family responsibilities, and other commitments taking up most of their time, finding a slot to squeeze in exercise can seem like an impossible task. As a result, many of them are unable to prioritise their physical health, which can have adverse effects on their overall well-being in the long run. Making time is so important, whether it is getting up half an hour earlier to go for a run before work or getting the bus to work or school drop off and running home. Instead of taking the dog for a walk, buy a running belt and run with the dog. Once you make these changes a regular part of your day or week you'll start to think "What did I used to do with my time?".

Self-Doubt: For many women, self-doubt can be a significant hurdle that keeps them from lacing up their running shoes. Negative thoughts and beliefs about their running ability can easily creep in and cause a lack of confidence, making it even more challenging to take that crucial first step. This self-doubt can be especially potent for those who are new to running or returning after an extended hiatus. The fear of not being able to keep up with others or meet self-imposed standards can be overwhelming and deter women from pursuing a potentially rewarding physical activity. It is essential to recognise these negative thoughts and beliefs as a barrier to progress and work to overcome them with a supportive and encouraging mindset. When we're out and about and see a runner go by we have no idea if that's their first ever run or if they've been running for years, quite honestly, we don't even care. It's the same when you take your first steps. No one knows it's your first run, take your time, put on your favourite playlist and go nice and slow. With time, patience, and perseverance, you will begin to build your confidence and develop a positive relationship with running.

Fear of Injury: For those who are new to running, the fear of getting injured can be a very real concern. Running is a high-impact activity that can put a lot of stress on the muscles and joints of the body, which can lead to a variety of injuries if proper precautions are not taken. These injuries can range from minor issues like muscle strains and sprains, to more serious problems like stress fractures or joint pain. It's important for beginners to take steps to prevent injury, such as gradually increasing the intensity and duration of their runs, wearing appropriate footwear, and stretching before and after each workout. By taking these precautions, beginners can minimise their risk of injury and enjoy the many benefits that running has to offer.

Practical Tips for Overcoming These Challenges

Time Management Strategies

Prioritise exercise: Incorporating running into your daily or weekly routine can greatly benefit your physical and mental health. One way to make sure you prioritise this activity is to schedule dedicated time for it, treating it as an essential appointment. This means setting aside a specific window of time each day or week solely for running, and not allowing other obligations or distractions to interfere with it. By doing so, you can establish a consistent running routine that becomes a regular part of your lifestyle and helps you stay active and healthy.

Make it convenient: When it comes to incorporating running into your daily routine, it's essential to choose routes and times that work well for you. It's recommended to select a running route that is convenient and safe, such as a park or a path that is well-lit and populated. Additionally, it's important to consider the time of day that works best for you. Some prefer to run in the early morning before work, while others may find it more convenient to go for a run during their lunch break or in the evening after work. By finding a time and route that fit seamlessly into your schedule, you'll be more likely to stick to your running routine and achieve your fitness goals.

Break it up: If you're having trouble finding a block of time to go for a full run, don't worry! You can break up your workout into shorter, more manageable segments throughout the day. For example, you might try going for a 10-minute run in the morning before work, another 10-minute run during your lunch break, and a final 10-minute run in the evening after dinner. This can be a great way to fit exercise into a busy schedule, and studies have shown that even short bursts of physical activity can have significant health benefits. So don't be discouraged if you can't find time for a full run – there are plenty of other ways to stay active and healthy!

Building Confidence

Set realistic goals: To start your fitness routine, it's important to set achievable goals. For instance, instead of aiming to run a marathon right away, start with a more reasonable goal, such as running for a certain distance or time. It's crucial to gradually increase the challenge as you progress, so your body has time to adapt to the new demands. This approach not only helps you avoid injury but also boosts your confidence and motivation to continue improving. Remember, consistency is key to achieving your fitness goals!

Focus on progress, not perfection: One of the best ways to stay motivated and on track towards your goals is to celebrate small victories and improvements that you make along the way. It's important to focus on the progress you've made, rather than dwelling on any setbacks or perceived shortcomings. When you acknowledge and celebrate your successes, no matter how small they may be, it helps to build your confidence, reinforces positive habits, and gives you the momentum you need to keep pushing forward. So, instead of getting discouraged by setbacks, take the time to recognise and appreciate the small steps you've taken towards your goals. It's a great way to stay motivated, build momentum, and stay on track towards success.

Surround yourself with support: If you're looking for ways to stay motivated and inspired to keep up with your running routine, seeking encouragement from friends, family, or running groups can be incredibly helpful. These are the people who know you best and understand the challenges you may be facing with your running. They can provide the kind of support that can help you stay on track, whether it's through words of encouragement, sharing their own experiences and ideas, or helping you stay accountable to your goals. In addition, running groups can offer a sense of community and camaraderie that can make the experience of running more enjoyable and fulfilling. So don't be afraid to reach out to those around you for their support and encouragement!

Injury Prevention Techniques

Invest in proper gear: It is important to wear running shoes that are supportive, fit well, and provide ample cushioning and stability to avoid injuries and ensure a comfortable running experience. To ensure that you are wearing the right shoes, it might be a good idea to consult with a professional at a specialist running store who can provide personalised recommendations based on your foot type, running gait, and other factors. They can also help you find shoes that provide the right amount of arch support, shock absorption, and flexibility for your specific needs. By investing in a good pair of running shoes that fit properly and offer the right support, you can enhance your running performance and minimise the risk of injury.

Warm-up and cool down: Before starting any physical activity or exercise routine, it's important to warm up your muscles and prepare your body for the upcoming challenge. Dynamic stretches are a great way to accomplish this. Dynamic stretches involve active movements that help to increase blood flow, elevate your heart rate, and loosen up your muscles. Examples of dynamic stretches include lunges, high knees, leg swings, and jumping jacks. Once you've finished your workout or physical activity, it's essential to cool down and stretch your muscles to prevent tightness and improve flexibility. This is where static stretches come into play. Static stretches involve holding a position for a certain amount of time, typically 20-30 seconds.

Examples of static stretches include hamstring stretches, quad stretches, and shoulder stretches. By incorporating static stretches into your post-workout routine, you'll be able to reduce your risk of injury, improve your overall flexibility, and help your body to recover more quickly.

Listen to your body: It is important to pay close attention to your body while running. Keep an eye out for any signs of discomfort or pain that may indicate an injury or overuse. If you start to feel any pain, adjust your pace or distance accordingly to prevent further harm. Incorporating rest days into your running routine is also crucial to allow your body to recover and reduce the risk of overuse injuries. Make sure to give yourself enough time to rest and recover between runs so that you can continue to improve your performance and maintain your overall health and well-being.

When it comes to developing a sustainable running routine, starting slow and gradually increasing intensity is crucial. The temptation to push yourself too hard or compare your progress to others should be avoided. Instead, it's important to focus on listening to your body, understanding its limits, and progressing at a pace that feels comfortable and manageable for you.

It's important to remember that every person is different and unique, and therefore every individual's running journey will be different. While some people may be able to run for longer periods of time with ease, others may need to start off with short runs and gradually build up their endurance. The key is to understand your body's abilities and limitations and work with them.

It's also vital to keep in mind that progress takes time, and it's okay to start off slow. In fact, starting off too aggressively can lead to injury, burnout, and ultimately, giving up on running altogether. Therefore, it's important to take small steps and celebrate every small victory along the way. Overall, the best approach to developing a sustainable running routine is to start slow, listen to your body, and progress at a pace that feels comfortable and manageable for you. Remember, every step forward, no matter how small, is a step in the right direction towards achieving your running goals. Remember there is no such thing as a bad run!

Chapter 4

From Couch to 5K: Building a Foundation

Are you interested in starting your running journey? Try the Couch to 5K program! If you are a beginner, starting a Couch to 5K program is an excellent way to ease into running gradually. It helps you build a strong foundation for your running journey. In this chapter, I will provide you with a complete guide on how to start a Couch to 5K program. We will also discuss the importance of proper footwear and clothing, and offer advice on finding motivation and staying consistent with training. Whether you are a fitness enthusiast or someone looking to improve your overall health, Couch to 5K program is an excellent choice for you.

What is a Couch to 5k Program?

A Couch to 5K program is a structured running plan designed for beginners who want to gradually build up their endurance and fitness levels. The program typically involves a series of workouts that gradually increase in intensity over a period of several weeks, with the ultimate goal of being able to run a 5K (or 3.1 miles) without stopping. The plan usually includes a combination of running and walking intervals, with the length of each interval gradually increasing as the week progresses. The program is a great way to get started with running, even if you've never run before, and can help you achieve your fitness goals in a safe and sustainable way.

Starting a Couch to 5K Program

If you're looking to get into running and don't know where to start, a Couch to 5K program is a great way to ease into it. Here's how you can begin:

Begin with Walk-Run Intervals: The first step is to alternate between walking and running intervals. Start with a ratio of 1 minute of running followed by 2-3 minutes of walking. This will allow your body to get used to the new routine. As time passes, gradually increase the duration of your running segments. Keep increasing the ratio until you can run continuously for 30 minutes or more. By following these steps, you'll be able to build up your endurance and complete a 5K in no time! Good luck!

Follow a Structured Plan: If you're looking to get into running and improve your fitness level, it's a good idea to follow a structured plan. There are many Couch to 5K programs available that provide detailed training plans, outlining specific workouts and progression goals for each week. By following a plan that aligns with your fitness level and goals, you can gradually increase the intensity and duration of your runs as you progress through the program. This will help you build up your endurance and improve your overall fitness level over time.

Some popular Couch to 5K programs includes:

1. C25K by Zen Labs

2. 5K Runner by Fitness22

3. Couch to 5K by Active Network

4. Ease into 5K by Bluefin Software

5. 5K Training by Red Rock Apps

Choose a program that suits your needs and preferences and stick to the structured plan to achieve your fitness goals.

Listen to Your Body: It is important to be mindful of your body's signals during and after each run. As you run, pay attention to any sensations of pain or discomfort, such as soreness, aching, or sharp twinges. If you feel any of these symptoms, it may be a sign that you are pushing yourself too hard or using improper form. To prevent injury, it is recommended that you take a break or adjust your intensity as needed. This could mean slowing down, decreasing your mileage or running frequency, or incorporating rest days into your routine. By listening to your body and making adjustments as necessary, you can avoid overuse injuries and stay healthy for the long term.

Rest and Recovery: Starting a new exercise routine can be exciting, but it's important to be mindful of your body's signals. It's normal to feel tired or sore after a workout, but if you experience extreme or persistent pain, it's a sign that you may be pushing yourself too hard. Rest and recovery are essential to prevent injury and allow your muscles to repair and grow. In fact, taking time to rest and recover is just as important as the physical activity itself. When starting a new exercise routine, it's important to start slowly and gradually build up your strength and endurance. Don't push yourself too hard, too fast, as this can lead to exhaustion or injury. Instead, focus on making small, consistent improvements over time. This could mean starting with a short walk or jog and gradually increasing your speed and distance each week. Remember to listen to your body and take breaks when necessary. Even scaling back your workouts, taking a day off, or incorporating restorative activities like yoga or stretching into your routine. By prioritising rest and recovery, you'll be able to achieve your fitness goals safely and sustainably. Happy running!

Importance of Proper Footwear and Clothing For Running

Tips for Choosing the Right Running Shoes

When it comes to running, having the right pair of shoes is crucial for a comfortable and enjoyable experience. During one of our runs together, a friend joined me for what was meant to be a casual outing. However, as we made our way back home, an unexpected mishap occurred. With each step, I noticed an odd flapping sound coming from my friend's feet. It wasn't until we arrived home that the source of the noise became clear—the soles of her trainers had entirely detached. Surprisingly, this wasn't the result of an intense, 6 hour-long run or a display of extraordinary speed. In fact, we had only been out for about twenty minutes. Instead, the culprit was her choice of footwear—old, worn-out shoes that had seen better days. It was a stark reminder of the importance of proper gear, even for seemingly brief activities like a short jog around the neighbourhood. From that day on, my friend learned the invaluable lesson (to never coming running with me again!) of investing in quality shoes for every run, no matter how short or leisurely it may seem.

Here are some ideas to help you choose the perfect pair:

Invest in quality shoes that provide adequate support, cushioning, and stability for your feet and ankles.

Consider visiting a specialty running store to get fitted for the right shoes based on your foot type, gait, and running style.

Try on several pairs and walk around in them to see how they feel before making your final decision.

Don't be swayed by fashion or brand names - prioritise comfort and performance over aesthetics.

Remember to replace your running shoes every 300 to 500 miles to ensure they continue to provide the necessary support and cushioning.

Running Clothing

When it comes to running, the right clothing can make all the difference. Here are some suggestions on what to wear for your next run:

To stay comfortable during your runs, choose fabrics that wick away moisture and allow your skin to breathe. This will help prevent discomfort caused by sweat buildup. Avoid cotton, as it can trap moisture and make you feel heavy and uncomfortable.

Dress in layers to accommodate changes in temperature and weather conditions. To stay comfortable during physical activity, start with a light and breathable layer underneath, then add a top that pulls moisture away from your body. If it's chilly outside, add a lightweight jacket or vest for added warmth.

Incorporating Hi-Vis clothing into your running gear can significantly reduce the risk of accidents, increase safety, and provide greater peace of mind when running in low-light conditions or high-traffic areas.

A good sports bra offers several benefits for women engaging in physical activities. A well-fitted sports bra can provide comfort by reducing chafing, irritation, and pressure on the shoulders, back, and chest during physical activities.

Good running socks offer several benefits that can enhance comfort, performance, and overall foot health during runs. These types of socks are designed with cushioning in key areas such as the heel, ball of the foot, and toe box. This extra padding provides shock absorption and support, reducing impact and minimising the risk of foot fatigue and injury. The seamless construction and specialised knitting techniques used in running socks help to minimise friction against the skin, reducing the likelihood of blisters and chafing, especially on long runs.

Running belts have become indispensable accessories for runners seeking convenience and functionality during their workouts. These sleek and lightweight belts offer a practical solution for storing essentials such as keys, phones, ID cards, and energy gels, allowing runners to focus solely on their performance without the distraction of carrying bulky items.

Wearing headphones and listening to music while running can offer several benefits. Music can serve as a powerful motivator, helping you push through fatigue. Upbeat and energetic songs can boost your mood and make your workout feel more enjoyable. With the vast variety of music available, you can create playlists that cater to your individual preferences and running goals. Whether you prefer high-energy tracks for intense workouts or calming melodies for a leisurely jog, you can tailor your music selection to suit your needs. It's important to consider safety concerns when wearing headphones while running outdoors. Make sure to keep the volume at a level where you can still hear potential hazards such as traffic or other runners and always remain aware of your surroundings. I prefer to wear Shokz headphones. These are open ear headphones; you can hear the music without blocking out ambient sounds.

Hats and Caps, these are of course a personal choice, but I like to run in a cap in the summer and a bobble hat in the winter.

By applying some of these ideas, you can ensure that you stay comfortable and focused during your runs.

Tips for Finding Motivation and Staying Consistent in Your Running Journey

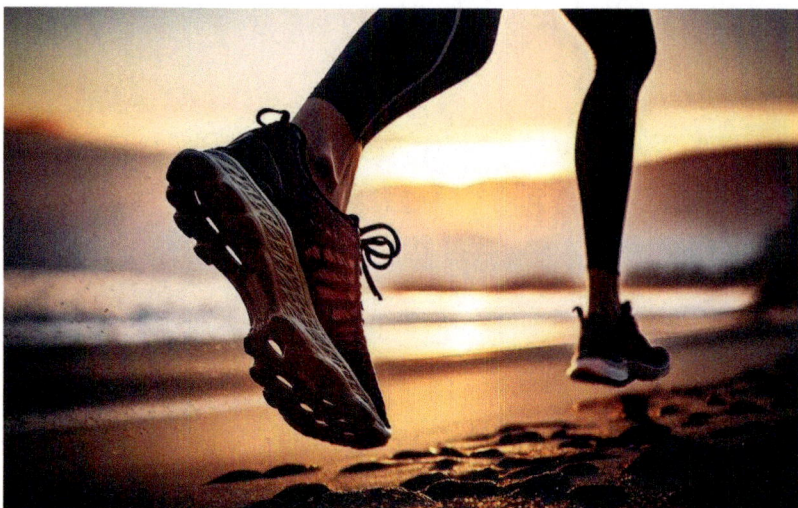

Whether you're just starting out with running or looking to improve your endurance and speed, staying motivated and consistent with your training can be a challenge. Here are some tips to help you set realistic goals, find a support system, mix up your workouts, and stay flexible with your training schedule:

Set Realistic Goals

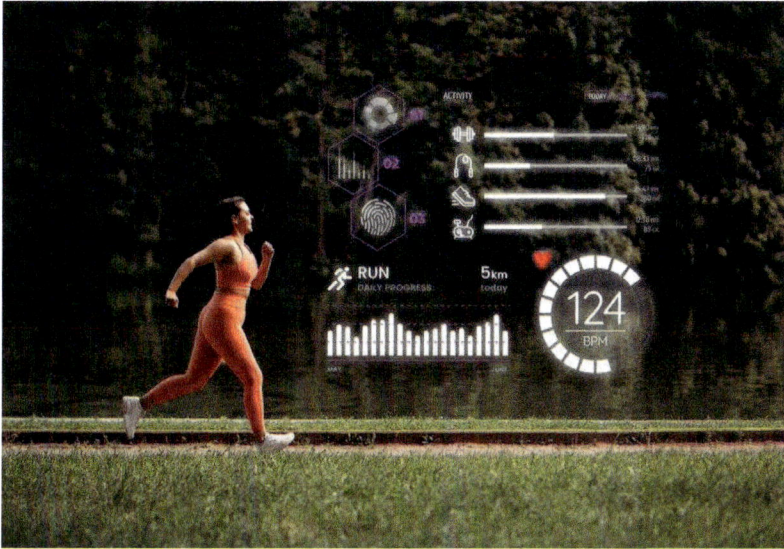

Setting achievable goals is essential for staying motivated and tracking your progress as a runner.

Start with a goal that is challenging but achievable. Whether it's completing your first 5K race or running a certain distance without stopping, choose a goal that excites and motivates you.

Break your goal down into smaller, manageable milestones. For example, if your goal is to run a 5K race, break it down into smaller milestones such as running for 10 minutes without stopping, then 15 minutes, and so on.

Celebrate your progress along the way. Take time to acknowledge and celebrate your achievements, no matter how small they may seem. This can help you stay motivated and on track with your training.

Find a Support System

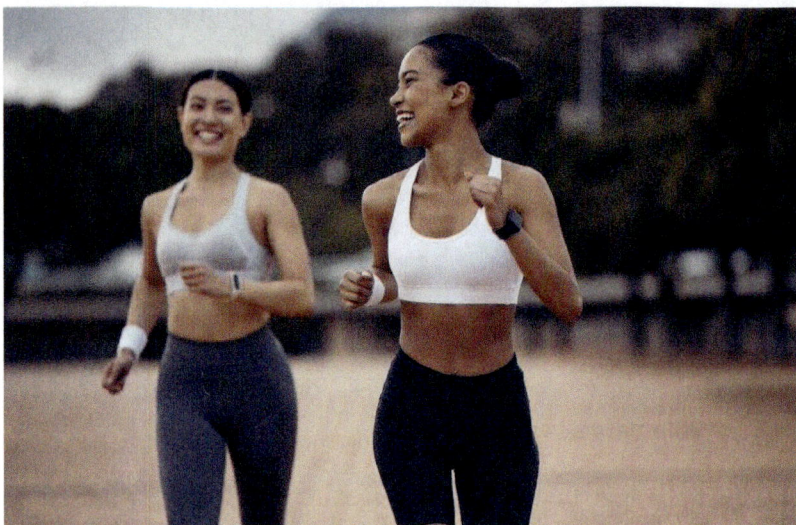

Having a support system can make all the difference when it comes to staying motivated and consistent with your running. I signed up for my second Marathon with my husband. Despite being a running long before I ever took it up, he had been sidelined by injuries for quite some time before training began and we weren't even sure he had a marathon in him but once our places were confirmed we both fully committed and knew we would do everything it takes to get us both over the finish line. Having someone sharing the same goal and mindset made an immense difference. Interestingly, we never trained together. We would plan our runs separately, sometimes leaving at the same time but heading in different directions. For me, it wasn't about having a running buddy; I cherished my solo running time. Instead it was about sharing a common interest and the mutual encouragement we offered each other before and after each run.

Thinking about finding a support system:

Surround yourself with supportive friends, family, or running buddies who can encourage and motivate you throughout your training. Having someone to share your successes and challenges with can help you stay accountable and motivated. You'll be surprised how many people are runners at work, in the office, your next door neighbour, mums at the school.

Joining a local running group or online community is a fantastic way to connect with fellow runners, whether you're a beginner or an experienced athlete. These groups offer invaluable support and accountability, along with a wealth of knowledge, tips, and advice. Running alongside individuals at similar levels allows for mutual learning and growth, fostering a strong sense of camaraderie. Together, you can push each other to reach new heights in your fitness journey, making the experience both enjoyable and rewarding.

Consider hiring a running coach or personal trainer to help you reach your goals and stay accountable. A coach can provide personalised training plans, feedback, and motivation to help you stay on track with your training.

Mix It Up

Keeping your runs interesting and enjoyable is essential for staying motivated and consistent with your training. Here are some tips for mixing up your workouts:

Vary your routes and scenery. Running the same route every day can become monotonous and boring. Try exploring new trails or parks to keep your runs interesting and enjoyable. Try running a familiar route in reverse. It's not always a race, stop, take pictures, enjoy the scenery, these runs are as much for your mental health as they are for the physical so take it all in.

Incorporate different types of workouts, such as interval training or hill repeats. These workouts can help improve your speed, endurance, and overall fitness, and can also help prevent boredom.

Experiment with different running surfaces, such as pavement, trails, or treadmills, to keep your workouts fresh and challenging. Running on different surfaces can also help prevent injury and improve your overall fitness. Treadmill running provides a convenient and controlled environment for runners to pursue their fitness goals regardless of weather conditions or time constraints. With adjustable speeds and inclines, treadmills offer versatility to accommodate various training needs and preferences. The cushioned surface of the treadmill deck helps reduce impact on joints, making it an ideal option for individuals seeking a low-impact workout. The joy of treadmill running is, if you've had enough, you will always finish where you started.

Stay Flexible

Staying flexible with your training schedule is essential for staying consistent with your running. Here are some tips for staying flexible:

Be flexible with your training schedule and adjust your workouts as needed to accommodate changes in your routine or unexpected obstacles. This can help prevent burnout and keep you motivated and on track with your training. Life is full of unexpected twists and turns—sudden meetings, impromptu errands, and unpredictable weather are all part of the mix. And that's perfectly okay. The key lies in not allowing one missed run to snowball into a pattern of inconsistency. It's easy to let one missed opportunity derail our entire routine but staying committed means bouncing back from setbacks with determination. Instead of dwelling on missed runs, focus on getting back on track as soon as possible. Consistency is the cornerstone of progress, and by staying resilient in the face of interruptions, we can maintain momentum towards our goals.

Remember that consistency is key, so aim to prioritise your runs and make them a regular part of your routine, even on busy days. Even a short run can help you maintain your fitness and stay motivated. If your plan is to run for 30 minutes today but you only manage to squeeze in 20, don't fret. Simply make up for the shortfall by adding the extra 10 minutes to your next run. Flexibility is key in maintaining a consistent workout routine, and adjusting your schedule to accommodate missed time ensures that you stay on track towards your fitness goals. By making up for missed minutes, you maintain progress and commitment to your running regimen, ultimately contributing to your overall fitness and well-being.

Listen to your body and take rest days when needed. Rest days are essential for allowing your body to recover and prevent injury. Perimenopause and menopause can indeed be exhausting, both physically and emotionally. While running can provide a much-needed boost of energy and vitality, it's important to listen to your body and prioritise rest when needed. Rest is an essential component of self-care, and by honouring your body's need for rest, you can better navigate the challenges of perimenopause and menopause while still enjoying the rejuvenating benefits of running.

By following these guidelines and staying committed to your running journey, you'll gradually build endurance, strength, and confidence as a runner, laying the foundation for future success and enjoyment in your running journey. Remember to stay motivated, be consistent, and have fun along the way!

Chapter 5

How to Take Your Running to the Next Level

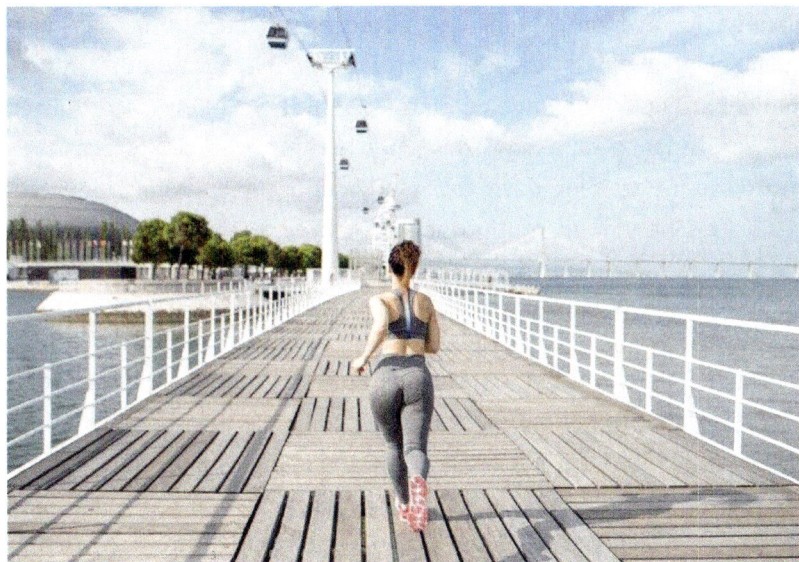

I never imagined myself running a marathon. Despite having been a runner for a few years, the challenges of perimenopause, coupled with crippling anxiety and impostor syndrome, made me doubt my capabilities. In fact, I hadn't even considered signing up for my first marathon—it was my husband who saw my potential and took the initiative to complete the registration on my behalf. Looking back, I'm grateful he did. Stepping into the realm of organised races was uncharted territory for me, but once committed, I knew there was no turning back. Armed with a 16-week training plan printed off the internet, I embarked on the journey with determination. Surprisingly, signing up for the event provided the push I needed to propel myself forward. It's a testament to the power of setting goals and embracing new challenges, even when self-doubt threatens to hold you back.

Sticking to a structured plan provided a welcomed relief from my anxiety. It gave me a sense of purpose and direction, offering a tangible focus amidst the chaos of perimenopause. Whether it was meticulously planning my upcoming runs in the evenings, scrutinising my performance data on Strava, or checking weather forecasts to strategise my training days, my mind was occupied with productive tasks. This newfound routine helped shift my attention away from the incessant worries that often overwhelmed me, allowing me to regain a sense of control and stability in my life.

Once I had completed my first Marathon, I was hooked. You spend many months preparing for the main event, filled with anticipation. You wonder what it will feel like, what the course will look like, and if you'll even be able to start, let alone finish. As you cross the start line, disbelief floods over you—how did you make it this far? The first few miles are pure joy, and as you pass the halfway mark, you're loving life. Then comes the struggle, pushing through miles 19, 20, and 21, convincing yourself you'll never do this again. By mile 23, with only a 5k to go, you tell yourself you're a champion. The finish line comes into view, and you think, just get me over it and I'm done—never to be repeated again. But as you cross the finish line, adrenaline surges through you, and all you can think is, "Wow, sign me up for another one."

Effective Strategies for Building Endurance and Improving Performance

I find running an excellent form of exercise that provides numerous health benefits, including improved cardiovascular health, weight management, stress relief, and more. However, to progress beyond the 5K distance and continue advancing as a runner, incorporating specific training strategies can help you build endurance and improve your overall performance. In this chapter, we'll discuss some effective strategies for taking your running to the next level:

Incorporate Interval Training: Interval training involves alternating between periods of high-intensity running and periods of lower-intensity recovery. This type of training can help improve your cardiovascular fitness, speed, and endurance. It's the slow, long runs that ultimately improve your overall endurance.

Sample workout: Warm up with 5-10 minutes of easy running, then alternate between 1-2 minutes of hard running (at a pace faster than your usual running pace) followed by 1-2 minutes of easy jogging or walking. Repeat this cycle for 20-30 minutes, then cool down with 5-10 minutes of easy running.

Incorporating interval training into your routine can help you break through plateaus and improve your running performance. By pushing your body to work at higher intensities, you'll boost your cardiovascular fitness, improve your running economy, and increase your lactate threshold, allowing you to run faster and longer.

Add Longer Runs to the Routine: Gradually increasing the distance of your runs is essential for building endurance and preparing your body for longer races. Incorporate one long run into your weekly training schedule, gradually increasing the distance over time. Start by adding 0.5-1 mile to your long run each week or increase the duration by 10-15 minutes. Aim to increase your long run distance by no more than 10-15% per week to avoid over-training and minimise the risk of injury. Adding longer runs to your routine can help you build endurance, improve your running form, and increase your mental toughness. By pushing through the discomfort and fatigue of longer runs, you'll develop the mental fortitude to tackle any challenges that come your way. The sense of achievement after a long run is quite extraordinary, serving as a powerful reminder of the progress made and the obstacles overcome. It's a culmination of perseverance, dedication, and resilience, leaving an indelible imprint on both the body and the mind.

Focus on Consistency: Consistency is key to making progress as a runner. Aim to run regularly, at least 3-4 times per week, to build and maintain your fitness level. Establish a weekly training schedule that includes a mix of easy runs, speed workouts, and long runs, with rest days or cross-training activities interspersed for recovery. Set specific, achievable goals for your training, whether it's completing a longer-distance race or improving your personal best time.

By sticking to a consistent training schedule, you'll give your body the stimulus it needs to adapt and grow stronger. You'll also develop the discipline and dedication required to achieve your running goals.

Honour your body's messages: Pay attention to how your body responds to training and adjust your workouts accordingly. It's normal to experience fatigue and muscle soreness, especially when increasing mileage or intensity, but be mindful of signs of overtraining or injury. Incorporate rest days or active recovery days into your training schedule to allow your body time to recover and repair. If you experience persistent pain or discomfort, scale back your training intensity or duration, and consider seeking advice from a qualified healthcare professional or running coach. By listening to your body and taking care of yourself, you'll avoid burnout and injury, allowing you to continue making progress and achieving your running goals.

Incorporating interval training, adding longer runs to your routine, focusing on consistency, and listening to your body, you'll be well-equipped to progress beyond the 5K distance and achieve your running goals. Remember to stay patient, stay motivated, and enjoy the journey as you continue to grow and evolve as a runner. With dedication, hard work, and smart training, you can take your running to the next level and achieve your full potential.

Why Cross-Training and Strength Training are Important for Runners

As a runner, you may have heard that cross-training and strength training are essential components of a versatile training regimen. But why are these activities so important? In this section, we'll explore the benefits of cross-training and strength training for runners, including injury prevention, improved performance, enhanced strength and power, injury rehabilitation and recovery, mental refreshment and motivation, and long-term health and longevity:

Injury Prevention

One of the biggest benefits of cross-training and strength training is injury prevention. Running is a high-impact exercise that can put a lot of stress on your joints and muscles. By incorporating other activities that target different muscle groups and movement patterns, you can improve overall muscle balance and reduce the risk of injury.

Some examples of cross-training activities that can complement running include swimming, cycling, or yoga. These activities provide low-impact cardiovascular conditioning, flexibility, and core strength. By adding these activities to your training regimen, you can help improve aerobic fitness, enhance endurance, and increase overall athleticism, translating to better performance on the roads or trails.

Improved Running Performance

In addition to injury prevention, cross-training activities can also improve your running performance. By providing additional cardiovascular conditioning and building strength in different muscle groups, cross-training can help you become a stronger, more well-rounded athlete. For example, swimming can be a great complement to running because it provides a low-impact cardiovascular workout that can help improve your lung capacity and overall endurance. Swimming is a low-impact exercise that offers a break from the repetitive stress of running. Immersion in water reduces the strain on joints and muscles, allowing for active recovery. Swimmers often experience improved flexibility and range of motion, which can help runners maintain better running form and prevent overuse injuries. Yoga, on the other hand, can help improve your flexibility and core strength, which can translate to better running form and improve running efficiency. Yoga also promotes mindfulness and mental focus through its emphasis on breath awareness and meditation. Runners who practise yoga often experience improved concentration, stress reduction, and better management of anxiety and race-day jitters. This mental clarity can lead to enhanced performance and a more enjoyable running experience.

Enhanced Muscular Strength and Power

Strength training is another important component of a balanced training program for runners. By developing stronger muscles, tendons, and ligaments, you can better withstand the repetitive stress of running and maintaining proper biomechanics. Some examples of exercises that can help improve leg strength, power, and stability include squats, lunges, dead-lifts, and plyometrics. By incorporating these exercises into your training regimen, you can improve your running mechanics and reduce fatigue, leading to better performance on the roads or trails.

Injury Rehabilitation and Recovery

Cross-training activities can also be beneficial during periods of injury rehabilitation or recovery. By allowing you to maintain cardiovascular fitness while giving your body a break from the repetitive impact of running, cross-training activities like swimming or cycling can help reduce stress on injured tissues. Of course, it's important to work with a healthcare provider or physical therapist to determine the best course of action during injury rehabilitation or recovery. However, incorporating cross-training activities into your routine can help you stay active and maintain fitness while you recover.

Mental Refreshment and Motivation

One of the biggest challenges of any training program is staying motivated and avoiding burnout. Incorporating cross-training and strength training into your routine can help add variety and diversity to your workouts, preventing boredom and burnout. I prefer to run alone so my weekly gym sessions with a friend not only keep me accountable but are so much fun. Mixing up your training routine can also challenge different muscle groups and provide a mental break from the monotony of running. This can lead to increased motivation and adherence to your training program, helping you achieve your goals and become a stronger athlete.

Longevity and Overall Health

Finally, cross-training and strength training can help improve your overall health and longevity. By diversifying your exercise routine with these activities, you can improve overall fitness, flexibility, and mobility, which are important for maintaining long-term health and longevity. Regular strength training has also been associated with reduced risk of chronic diseases such as osteoporosis, diabetes, and cardiovascular disease. By incorporating strength training into your routine, you can help reduce your risk of these diseases and maintain overall health and wellness.

Thus, cross-training and strength training are invaluable components of a well-rounded training program for runners. By incorporating these activities into your routine, you can enjoy benefits such as injury prevention, improved performance, enhanced strength and power, injury rehabilitation and recovery, mental refreshment and motivation, and long-term health and longevity. If you're new to cross-training or strength training, it's important to start slowly and work with a qualified trainer or coach to develop a program that's right for you. With time and dedication, you can become a stronger, more resilient athlete, both on and off the roads or trails.

Challenges in Running: Strategies to Overcome Pacing and Nutrition Issues

Running is one of the most popular forms of exercise for people of all ages. It can improve mental health, boost cardiovascular endurance, and enhance overall fitness. However, increasing distance and speed in running can introduce several common challenges that can impact performance and overall well-being. Two significant factors to consider are pacing and nutrition.

Pacing Challenges

One common challenge encountered when increasing distance and speed in running is pacing, or the delicate balance between pushing oneself too hard and risking exhaustion, versus holding back and not pushing hard enough. Striking the right balance is crucial: running too fast can result in premature fatigue, and potential injury, while running too slowly may impede progress and fail to provide the necessary stimulus for improvement. To surmount pacing challenges, it's imperative to attune yourself to your body's signals and develop a keen sense of your effort level. Factors such as breathing rhythm, heart rate variability, and perceived exertion can serve as valuable guides. Utilising a running watch equipped with various tracking metrics can further aid in monitoring these parameters during your run, offering real-time feedback to help you adjust your pace and effort accordingly.

Structured Workouts

Incorporating structured workouts such as interval training, tempo runs, and long runs with varying paces can help you develop a sense of pacing and improve your ability to sustain faster speeds over longer distances.

Interval Training

Interval training is a type of workout that involves alternating periods of high-intensity effort with periods of lower intensity or rest. It helps build endurance, speed, and power. A typical interval training workout involves running at maximum effort for a set amount of time, followed by a period of rest or lower-intensity exercise. The duration and intensity of each interval can vary depending on your fitness level and training goals.

Tempo runs are designed to help you improve your lactate threshold, which is the point at which your body begins to produce more lactic acid than it can clear. By running at a steady pace that is slightly faster than your comfortable pace, you can train your body to become more efficient at clearing lactic acid and improving your endurance.

Long runs are an essential part of any distance runner's training program. They help build endurance, improve cardiovascular fitness, and prepare your body for the physical demands of long-distance running. To build your endurance, start with a comfortable distance and gradually increase the length of your long runs over time.

Additionally, using tools such as GPS watches or smartphone apps can help you track your pace and monitor your progress during training sessions. They can also help you stay motivated and accountable by tracking your progress over time and providing feedback on your performance.

Nutrition Challenges

Proper nutrition is critical for fuelling your body and supporting optimal performance during long-distance and high-intensity running. One challenge faced by runners is ensuring adequate energy intake to support increased training demands without overeating or consuming unhealthy foods.

Runners during menopause can present unique hurdles due to hormonal changes, altered metabolism, and potential shifts in dietary preferences. Managing these challenges effectively is essential for maintaining energy levels, supporting overall health, and optimising performance. Ageing and hormonal changes can contribute to the loss of muscle mass, which may impact running performance and overall strength. Prioritise protein intake to support muscle repair and growth. Menopause can also impact nutrient absorption and utilisation, leading to deficiencies in essential vitamins and minerals. Incorporate a variety of nutrient-dense foods into your diet to ensure adequate intake of vitamins and minerals. Consider supplementation if needed but consult with a healthcare professional first.

It's essential to fuel your body with a balanced diet that includes a variety of nutrient-dense foods, including carbohydrates, protein, healthy fats, vitamins, and minerals. A balanced diet can provide the necessary nutrients to support your training and recovery while maintaining optimal health and well-being.

In the next chapter, we will explore nutrition in greater detail.

By addressing pacing and nutrition challenges head-on and implementing strategies to overcome them, you can enhance your running performance, improve endurance, and achieve your distance and speed goals while maintaining optimal health and well-being. Remember to approach training with patience, consistency, and a focus on gradual progression to minimise the risk of injury and maximise long-term success. Running is a journey, and with the right mindset, tools, and strategies, you can achieve your goals and enjoy the many benefits of this rewarding form of exercise.

Chapter 6

Comprehensive Guide on How to Optimise Nutrition and Hydration for Running Performance

As I have already mentioned, running is a fantastic way to stay fit and healthy, but it takes a lot of energy and effort. Proper nutrition and hydration play crucial roles in running performance and recovery, impacting energy levels, endurance, muscle function, and overall well-being. Here's a comprehensive guide on how to optimise nutrition and hydration before, during, and after your runs.

Pre-Run Nutrition

What you eat before a run can have a significant impact on your performance. It's essential to consume a balanced meal or snack containing carbohydrates, protein, and a small amount of healthy fats 1-2 hours before your run.

Carbohydrates provide the primary fuel source for running, so focus on foods such as whole grains, fruits, vegetables, and legumes. These foods are easily digestible and provide sustained energy throughout the run.

Include a moderate amount of protein to support muscle repair and recovery, such as lean meats, poultry, fish, eggs, dairy products, tofu, or legumes. Protein helps repair and rebuild muscles and aids in recovery.

It's best to avoid foods high in fat, fibre, or sugar, which can cause gastrointestinal discomfort during exercise. These foods take longer to digest, and they can cause bloating, cramping, and other issues.

Stay hydrated by drinking water or a sports drink leading up to your run, but avoid consuming large amounts of fluid immediately before running to prevent bloating or discomfort.

Some examples of what to eat would be:

Overnight oats are a convenient and nutritious option for fuelling your long run, providing a balance of carbohydrates, protein, and healthy fats to sustain energy levels.

Whole grain toast offers complex carbohydrates, while scrambled eggs provide high-quality protein. Top it off with sliced avocado for healthy fats and additional nutrients. This meal provides a good mix of macronutrients to sustain energy levels during your run.

Greek yoghurt is rich in protein and probiotics, while berries offer antioxidants and carbohydrates. Add some granola for crunch and extra carbs. This meal is light yet nutritious, providing protein for muscle repair and carbohydrates for energy.

Remember to fuel up on plenty of carbohydrates the night before a long run. Pizza and pasta are my go-to meals.

Before you run, it's important to ensure you hydrate by drinking water or a sports drink but avoid consuming large amounts of fluid immediately before to prevent bloating or discomfort.

During-Run Nutrition

During longer runs, consider using sports drinks, energy gels, or other portable fuel sources to replenish carbohydrates and electrolytes and maintain energy levels. Sports drinks can provide carbohydrates and electrolytes, which are essential for maintaining hydration and energy levels during prolonged exercise. Energy gels are convenient and portable sources of carbohydrates that can provide an energy boost during long runs or intense workouts.

Portable fuel sources such as energy gels, chews, or sports drinks can provide easily digestible carbohydrates and electrolytes to support endurance and performance.

For runs lasting longer than 60-90 minutes I work on the one sports gel every 5k or every 30 minutes premise.

Incorporating sports gels at regular intervals to sustain energy levels and hydration. Sports gels are a convenient and effective way to replenish carbohydrates and electrolytes during endurance exercise, helping to prevent fatigue and maintain performance. Choosing sports gels without caffeine is a personal preference and may be the right decision for you based on your individual needs and preferences. While caffeine can provide an additional energy boost and enhance mental focus, some individuals may be sensitive to its effects or prefer to avoid it altogether.

Non-caffeinated sports gels still provide a source of carbohydrates and electrolytes to fuel your long runs without the added stimulant. They can be just as effective at replenishing glycogen stores, delaying fatigue, and supporting hydration during exercise. Plus, opting for non-caffeinated gels can help prevent potential side effects such as jitteriness, increased heart rate, or disrupted sleep patterns that some individuals may experience with caffeine consumption. Ultimately, the most important factor is finding what works best for you and supports your performance and enjoyment of running. Experiment with different types of sports gels during training runs to determine which ones you prefer and how they affect your energy levels and overall performance.

Remember, stay hydrated by sipping water or a sports drink regularly throughout your run, especially in hot or humid conditions. Dehydration can impair performance and increase fatigue, so it's essential to stay hydrated during the run.

Post-Run Nutrition

After a run, it's essential to replenish your body's glycogen stores and support muscle recovery by consuming a balanced meal or snack containing carbohydrates and protein within 30-60 minutes. Aim for a 3:1 or 4:1 ratio of carbohydrates to protein to optimise recovery, such as a smoothie with fruit and Greek yoghurt, a turkey sandwich on whole-grain bread, or a bowl of oatmeal topped with nuts and berries.

Include sources of antioxidants and anti-inflammatory nutrients to help reduce exercise-induced inflammation and promote recovery, such as fruits, vegetables, nuts, seeds, and fatty fish. These foods contain essential nutrients that aid in recovery and reduce inflammation.

Drink plenty of fluids to replace sweat losses and rehydrate your body. Water is typically sufficient for shorter runs, while longer or more intense workouts may warrant the use of a sports drink to replace electrolytes lost through sweat.

Pay attention to your body's signals and adjust your nutrition plan based on individual preferences, dietary restrictions, and training goals. Experiment with different foods and supplements to find what works best for you. Keep a food diary to track your intake and identify any patterns or deficiencies.

Importance of Staying Hydrated

Proper hydration is essential for maintaining blood volume, regulating body temperature, transporting nutrients, and supporting muscle function during exercise. Dehydration can impair performance, increase fatigue, and elevate the risk of heat-related illnesses such as heat exhaustion or heatstroke.

Monitor your fluid intake and aim to drink water or a sports drink regularly throughout the day. It's essential to stay hydrated throughout the day, not just during exercise. I really struggle to get enough water in me.

Pay attention to thirst cues and urine colour to gauge hydration status, aiming for pale yellow urine and drinking enough fluids to stay adequately hydrated. Dark yellow urine indicates dehydration, and it's essential to drink more fluids to maintain proper hydration.

Strategies for Maintaining Proper Hydration Levels

Drink water or a sports drink before, during, and after your runs to replace fluid losses and prevent dehydration. Drinking fluids before, during, and after running is essential to stay hydrated and maintain proper fluid balance.

Hydrate consistently throughout the day, aiming for a total fluid intake of at least 8-10 cups (64-80 ounces) per day, or more if you're exercising intensely or in hot weather. Constantly drinking fluids throughout the day is essential for staying hydrated.

Consider weighing yourself before and after your runs to estimate sweat losses and determine your hydration needs. Aim to replace lost fluids by drinking 16-24 ounces of fluid for every pound of body weight lost during exercise.

Monitor environmental conditions such as temperature, humidity, and altitude, as these factors can increase fluid needs and elevate the risk of dehydration. Environmental factors affect fluid needs, and it's essential to adjust fluid intake accordingly.

Be mindful of individual factors such as sweat rate, sodium losses, and urine output, and adjust your hydration strategy accordingly to maintain proper fluid balance and optimise performance. Individual factors affect fluid needs, and it's essential to adjust fluid intake accordingly.

By prioritising nutrition and hydration before, during, and after your runs, you can support optimal performance, enhance recovery, and maximise the benefits of your training efforts. Experiment with different foods, fluids, and timing to find what works best for your body and individual needs and listen to your body's cues to ensure you're adequately fuelled and hydrated for every run. Remember to stay hydrated throughout the day, not just during exercise, and adjust your fluid intake according to individual and environmental factors. With proper nutrition and hydration, you can achieve your running goals and stay healthy and fit.

The Connection Between Running and Mental Health: Tips for Managing Stress and Anxiety

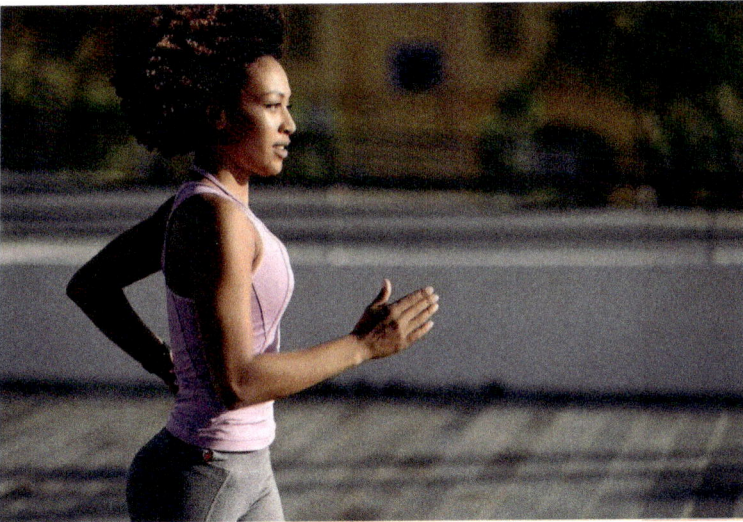

Running can have a profound impact on mental health. Many studies have highlighted the positive effects of running on emotional well-being, such as reducing stress and anxiety, improving mood, and promoting overall mental resilience. Here's an exploration of the connection between running and mental health, along with tips for managing stress and anxiety through running:

Stress Relief

Running can be an effective natural outlet for releasing stress and tension accumulated throughout the day. Through the rhythmic motion of running, combined with the release of endorphins, known as "feel-good" hormones, it can help reduce levels of stress hormones such as cortisol and promote feelings of relaxation and calm. Engaging in regular running can provide a much-needed break from the demands and pressures of daily life, allowing you to clear your mind, gain perspective, and recharge both physically and mentally.

Here are some tips to make running a stress-relieving activity:

Schedule regular runs into your weekly routine and prioritise them as essential self-care activities.

Choose running routes that bring you joy and inspiration, whether it's a scenic trail, a peaceful park, or your favourite neighbourhood streets. If you're lucky enough to live by the sea and run along a beach can be both challenging and also invigorating.

Pay attention to how running affects your mood and stress levels, and adjust your pace, distance, and intensity accordingly. Respect your body's limits and avoid pushing yourself too hard, especially during times of heightened stress or fatigue.

Mood Enhancement

Running has been shown to improve mood and alleviate symptoms of depression and anxiety. The release of endorphins during exercise can elevate mood, boost energy levels, and enhance overall emotional well-being. Regular running can also increase levels of neurotransmitters such as serotonin and dopamine, which are associated with feelings of happiness and pleasure, contributing to improved mood and mental health.

Here are some tips to make running a mood-enhancing activity:

Start with shorter, gentler runs if you're new to running or dealing with high levels of stress or anxiety, and gradually increase intensity and duration as you build confidence and resilience.

Incorporate mindfulness techniques such as deep breathing, visualisation, or body scanning to enhance the therapeutic effects of running and promote a greater sense of calm and balance.

Consider joining a local running group or online community to connect with like-minded individuals who share your passion for running and mental health.

Stress Management

Running serves as a powerful coping mechanism for managing stress and anxiety. Engaging in physical activity can help shift focus away from negative thoughts and worries, allowing you to channel your energy into something productive and uplifting. Establishing a regular running routine provides a sense of structure and consistency, which can be particularly beneficial during times of uncertainty or upheaval.

Here are some ideas to make running a stress-management activity:

Set small, achievable goals for your runs to provide a sense of accomplishment and control, boosting self-confidence and resilience in the face of stressors.

Treat your running time as non-negotiable and protect it from other obligations or distractions.

Tune into your breath, body sensations, and surroundings to cultivate a sense of mindfulness during your runs, allowing you to let go of past regrets and future worries and focus on the here and now.

Mindfulness and Presence

Running offers an opportunity to practise mindfulness and present-moment awareness. By tuning into your breath, body sensations, and surroundings, you can cultivate a sense of mindfulness during your runs, allowing you to let go of past regrets and future worries and focus on the here and now. Incorporating mindfulness techniques such as deep breathing, visualisation, or body scanning can enhance the therapeutic effects of running and promote a greater sense of calm and balance.

Here are some suggestions to make running a mindfulness and presence activity:

Choose a time of day when you're most alert and can fully engage in your run.

Start with a few minutes of deep breathing or visualisation to help you get present and focused.

Notice your surroundings and appreciate the beauty and serenity of nature or the cityscape around you.

Running offers a powerful antidote to stress and anxiety, providing a natural outlet for releasing tension, boosting mood, and promoting overall mental well-being. By incorporating regular running into your routine and implementing strategies for managing stress and anxiety, you can harness the impacts of running to cultivate resilience, balance, and inner peace in your life.

Chapter 7

Things I've learnt on my running journey.

When to start? The time to start is now! Put on your running shoes and step outside, even if it's for 5 minutes. Running is free, you don't need to worry about expensive monthly memberships or booking introductory appointments. Just lace up your trainers, open the front door, and embrace the fresh air on your skin. Once you get started you won't regret it.

There's no such thing as a bad run. Even if you're running the slowest 5K, you're still faster than someone sitting on the couch. Pace and distance are irrelevant: any distance you cover is a run. Your only competition is with yourself. Don't let other people or social media define what kind of runner you are. A marathon is 26.2 miles, and both the person who comes first and the person who finishes last are marathon runners.

You'll never regret a run. Whether it's a challenging day where every step feels heavy or a day where you feel like you're flying effortlessly, each run adds to your journey and growth. The feeling of accomplishment, the clarity of mind and the rush of endorphins make every run worthwhile. Even on the toughest days, getting out there and moving your body brings its own kind of satisfaction. So lace up those shoes and hit the pavements or trails - your future self will thank you.

Run to eat cake! While running certainly helps with weight control, I've learnt not to get hung up on the numbers on the dreaded scales. Regular exercise maintains a healthy weight, so run for that cake, chocolate, glass of wine, whatever makes you feel good without worrying about the extra calories. I follow many inspiring women online who run for the joy of it and not to lose weight. Personally, I run mostly for the remarkable impact it has on my mind. So if you want a treat as an after run reward, go for it!!

Have fun running!! Don't take it too seriously. Instead of comparing and analysing, let's make it a fun part of our day. Enjoy the music, enjoy the company, even if you only have yourself for company. Revel in the scenery and the fresh air. Appreciate that you're doing something amazing for yourself. Embrace the moment and savour every step.

Running won't magically solve your problems, but it can be a powerful tool for coping with them. It has certainly been a game changer for my anxiety and worries. The solitude (something I once hated) allows me to process things without the distractions of daily questions like "What's for dinner?" or "Have you seen the TV remote?". It's a chance to escape the confines of four walls, to be outdoors and breathe in the fresh air. Sometimes, it's not about processing anything but simply being alone and embracing the moment.

The body is a powerful machine, a wonderful gift that keeps going over and over again until we tell it to stop. Have faith in your body, it will always follow your lead. However, the mind is where we often face challenges. It's the mind that impedes our progress, whispering "Stop, I can't do this", long before the body gives up. So, it's just as important to work on strengthening the mind to keep pushing forward. When the mind is strong and determined, the body will follow suit.

How I feel when running:

Mile 1 - Awful! Hate it, make it stop! Why am I doing this? I should be doing a million other things. Why? Why, why?

Mile 2 - This isn't so bad. I can actually breathe and focus on my steps. Life isn't so bad after all.

Mile 3 - I am a beast! Watch me go! I've just overtaken an old lady pushing a shopping trolley. I can hear Chariots of fire ringing in my ears. I am alive!!

The ugly side of running

Navigating the less glamorous aspects of running, let's talk about toenails. Who really needs them anyway? Here's the lowdown: if you're easing into running with a goal like a 5K and hitting the pavement a few times a week, your toenails will likely stay intact. However, if you start feeling any discomfort, it's time to take action. Trim those toenails really short to avoid any potential issues. As mentioned above, when it comes to footwear, invest in a pair that's half a size bigger than your usual size. This gives your feet room to breathe and prevents your toenails from getting jammed against the front of the shoe. Quality socks are a game-changer too; they can reduce friction and provide additional cushioning. Speaking from personal experience, after my first marathon, I said goodbye to all but my big toenails. It wasn't exactly a sight to behold, but I was logging serious miles week after week. So, if you're sticking to a few 5K's a week, you should be in the clear. Just remember, take care of those feet!

Your bowels Lie!! They can be quite deceptive, making you believe you're all set before a run when, in reality, you're not. Trust me on this one: you do need that pre-run pit stop. Our bodies have a sneaky knack for convincing us that everything's in order, only to pull a fast one on us just a mile into our run. Suddenly, the urge hits, and you're left regretting not heeding the call earlier.

So, do yourself a favour and take that extra 5 minutes before heading out the door. Trust me, you'll thank yourself once you're on the road without any unexpected detours to the nearest toilet. It's a small step that can make a big difference in your running experience!

Chafing: the uncomfortable truth that can strike anyone, regardless of size. It's real, it hurts, and it's a runner's nemesis. One of the best ways to combat chafing is to be mindful of your clothing choices.

Avoid running in shorts or pants with seams that rub against your inner thighs. Those seams can become a constant source of irritation, leading to chafing. Instead, opt for longer leggings or seamless designs that minimise friction. Another helpful tip is to use skin lubricants or roll-on's specifically designed for sports. These products create a protective barrier between your skin and clothing, reducing the risk of chafing.

The last thing you want is to be halfway through your run and find yourself sidelined by pain or discomfort. So, take these precautions to ensure a more comfortable and enjoyable running experience. After all, pain-free miles are the best kind of miles!

Taking care of your nipples might not be the first thing on your mind when you're gearing up for a run, but trust me, it's important! While a good sports bra can provide adequate support, it's not always enough to prevent nipple chafing. I've even seen my husband peel off half his nipple from his sports vest, and let me tell you, it's not a sight you want to see—or experience. This kind of discomfort usually occurs when there isn't sufficient protection between your skin and the fabric of your top. So, what's the solution? Consider using nipple guards or lubricants designed specifically to prevent chafing. These products can create a barrier and reduce friction, keeping your nipples comfortable and intact during your runs. Remember, a little prevention goes a long way. So, look after those nipples and make sure they're well-protected before you hit the road or trail. Your nipples will thank you!

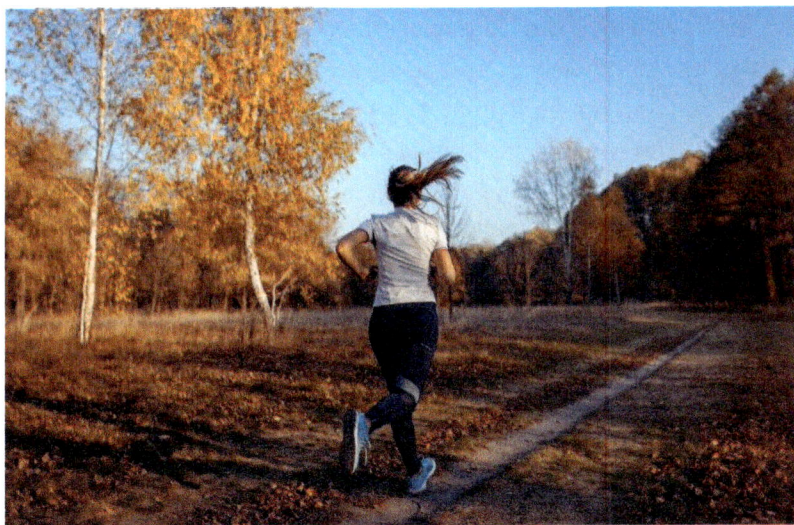

Conclusion

Throughout the pages of this book, we have explored the benefits of running as a tool for managing the challenges of menopause and finding empowerment with every stride. From the physical and mental health benefits to the strategies for managing stress and anxiety, let's recap the main points covered in this book. Running is a fantastic way to improve cardiovascular health, manage weight, reduce stress, enhance mood, and increase confidence. Regular exercise, such as running, can help reduce the risk of chronic diseases like type 2 diabetes, heart disease, and some cancers. Running can also be an effective way to manage menopausal symptoms such as hot flashes, mood swings, and sleep disturbances. As a low-impact activity, running can be a great way to increase bone density, which is essential for women in menopause. Moreover, running offers a sense of accomplishment and achievement that can help boost self-confidence and self-esteem.

If you're a beginner, starting a Couch to 5K (C25K) program can provide a structured approach to gradually build endurance and confidence as a runner. A C25K program involves a combination of walking and running intervals, with the goal of gradually increasing the running intervals while decreasing the walking intervals. This approach can help you avoid injury and build your fitness level at a sustainable pace. There are numerous C25K programs available online, and many running apps offer this training plan.

Proper nutrition and hydration are essential for fuelling performance, supporting recovery, and maintaining overall health and well-being before, during, and after runs. Eating a balanced diet that includes a variety of whole foods, including fruits, vegetables, lean protein, and whole grains, can provide your body with the nutrients it needs to perform at its best. Hydration is also crucial, especially when running in hot weather. Drink water before, during, and after your runs to stay hydrated.

Running can be an effective way to manage stress and anxiety. Prioritising self-care, finding joy in the journey, and connecting with a supportive community are strategies that can help you get the most out of your running experience. Self-care includes getting enough rest, taking time to stretch, and listening to your body. Finding joy in the journey involves focusing on the process rather than the outcome. It can mean enjoying nature, listening to music or a podcast, or simply taking in the surroundings. Furthermore, connecting with a supportive community can provide accountability, motivation, and encouragement.

As we age, it's essential to prioritise our health and well-being, especially during menopause. Running can be a valuable tool for navigating menopause and reclaiming control of your health and happiness. By incorporating running into your lifestyle, you can improve your physical and mental health, reduce stress, and boost your confidence. Remember that every step you take towards fitness and well-being, no matter how small, is a significant achievement worthy of celebration.

Whether you're completing a 5K, a marathon, or simply lacing up your shoes and hitting the pavement, each moment spent running is an opportunity for growth, empowerment, and self-discovery. It's essential to celebrate your achievements, no matter how small they are. Running can be a challenging activity, and it's crucial to acknowledge and celebrate your progress.

As you continue on your running routine, it's important to keep moving forward, one step at a time. Remember that the road ahead is yours to conquer. Set achievable goals, challenge yourself, and push yourself out of your comfort zone. Running can be a powerful tool for personal growth and development, and it's essential to embrace the journey.

Running can be an effective tool for navigating menopause and finding empowerment with every stride. From the physical and mental health benefits to the strategies for managing stress and anxiety, running can help you take control of your health and well-being. Remember to celebrate your achievements, keep moving forward, and embrace the experience. Happy running, and may you find delight in every stride.

I truly believe running has saved my life. Perimenopause and Menopause can be a lonely and scary place and I don't know where I would be if I didn't have running in my life. Not only do I feel I've found myself again but I've also found a person that I didn't even know existed within me. A stronger, determined woman who wants to keep on improving.

Claire Kyriacou x

References

1. Pfitzinger, P., & Douglas, S. (2019). Advanced Marathoning. Human Kinetics.

2. Noakes, T. (2012). Lore of Running (4th ed.). Human Kinetics.

3. Galloway, J. (2014). Galloway's Book on Running. Meyer & Meyer Sport.

4. Fitzgerald, M. (2014). 80/20 Running: Run Stronger and Race Faster by Training Slower. Penguin Random House.

5. Matt, F. (2017). Running Rewired: Reinvent Your Run for Stability, Strength, and Speed. VeloPress.

6. Benson, J., & Stein, P. (2016). The Runner's Edge: High-tech Training for Peak Performance. Human Kinetics.

7. Magness, S. (2014). The Science of Running: How to Find Your Limit and Train to Maximize Your Performance. Origin Press.

8. Karp, J. (2014). Running for Women. Human Kinetics.

9. Higdon, H. (2011). Marathon: The Ultimate Training Guide. Rodale Books.

10. Murakami, H. (2009). What I Talk About When I Talk About Running. Vintage International.

11. Clark, R., & Lucett, S. (2014). NASM Essentials of Sports Performance Training. Lippincott Williams & Wilkins.

12. Bernd Heinrich. (2002). Why We Run: A Natural History. HarperCollins.

13. Parker-Pope, T. (2009). The New York Times Book of Health: How to Feel Fitter, Eat Better, and Live Longer. St. Martin's Griffin.

14. Tudor-Locke, C., & Bassett, D. R. (2004). How Many Steps/Day Are Enough? For Adults. Sports Medicine, 34(1), 1–8.

15. Hutchinson, A. (2018). Endure: Mind, Body, and the Curiously Elastic Limits of Human Performance. William Morrow.

Printed in Great Britain
by Amazon